REAL-LIFE MONSTERS
CREATURES
OF THE DEEP

THE WORLD'S
WEIRDEST
WATER DWELLERS

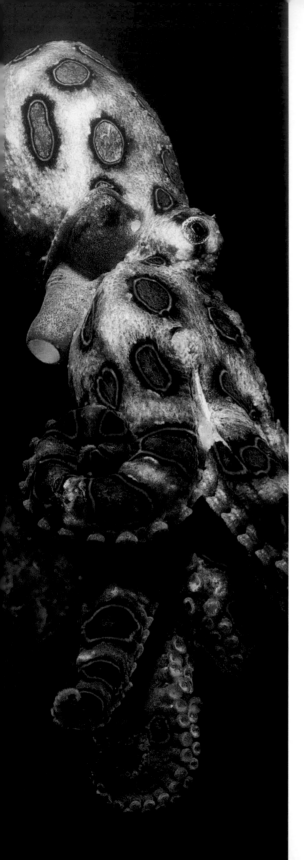

Thanks to the creative team:
SeniorEditor: AliceP eebles
Designer: Lauren Woods and collaborate agency

Hungry Tomato™
A division of Lerner Publishing Group, Inc.
241F irst Avenue North
Minneapolis, MN 55401 USA

For reading levels and more information, look up this title at www.lernerbooks.com.

Main body text set in Century Gothic Regular 9.5/11.4
Typeface provided by Monotype Typography

Library of Congress Cataloging-in-Publication Data

The Cataloging-in-Publication Data for *Creatures of the Deep* is on file at the Library of Congress.
ISBN 978-1-4677-6360-8 (lib. bdg.)
ISBN978-1-4677-7643-1 (pbk.)
ISBN 978-1-4677-7227-3 (EB pdf)

Manufactured in the United States of America
2-46849-18261-4/6/2021

REAL-LIFE MONSTERS
CREATURES OF THE DEEP

By Matthew Rake

Illustrated by Simon Mendez

HUNGRY
TOMATO™

Minneapolis

CONTENTS

We live on a planet that is covered with 139 million square miles (361 million square kilometers) of water. Water makes up over 70 percent of the world's surface and, at its deepest, goes as deep as 6.8 miles (11 km). Have you ever thought about what sort of monsters lurk in all that water? Well, you are about to find out. Most animals live at the surface of the ocean where the sunlight can penetrate. However, in this book, we will go down to the cold, dark depths to find some of the scariest, most sinister, and downright ugly creatures on the planet.

No light can penetrate more than 3,280 feet (1,000 meters) down, and below that is called the midnight zone. It's here, in mysterious darkness, that the goblin shark, many species of anglerfish, and the blobfish all lurk. The goblin shark catches prey with amazing jaws that catapult forward. The anglerfish has a more subtle approach: it lures prey toward itself with what looks like bait on the end of a fishing rod.

A bit higher in the ocean, about 650 to 3,280 feet (200 to 1,000 m) deep, some sunlight penetrates the water. This is known as the twilight zone. Here the giant squid hangs out, ready to reach out its 33-foot-long (10 m) tentacles to snatch any unsuspecting sea life passing by.

Great white sharks can also dive down into the twilight zone, but they usually live in the sunlight zone in the top 650 feet (200 m) of the water. Here great whites can find their favorite meals: juicy seals and sea lions.

Killer whales also inhabit this zone, eating everything from other whales, dolphins, and sharks to small fish such as herring and salmon. Together, great whites and killer whales are the ocean's top predators.

In the sunlight zone, you will also find blue-ringed octopi, cone snails, sarcastic fringeheads, and moray eels, all living in reefs or near the shore. The blue-ringed octopus, with its wonderful color, and cone snail, with its pretty, patterned shell, might look harmless, but beware! They are two of the most poisonous creatures in the animal kingdom. And you don't want to go anywhere near a sarcastic fringehead or a moray eel—they have razor-sharp teeth and a powerful bite. Morays have even been known to bite off divers' fingers.

So if you're ready to plunge into the world of marine monsters, jump right in . . .

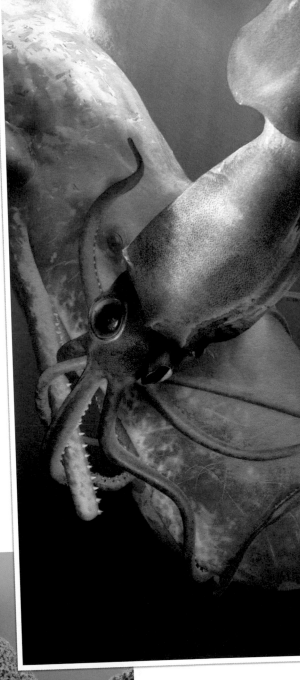

BLOBFISH

Length: up to 12 in (30 cm)
Weight: 21 lb (9.5 kg)
Location: off the shores of southeastern
Australia and New Zealand

Most fish have a swim bladder. It's simply a gas-filled organ inside the body that helps them stay buoyant. The blobfish, however, lives at depths of 2,000 to 3,900 feet (600 to 1,200 m) and the swim bladder doesn't work too well down there. The water pressure is more than one hundred times higher than it is at the surface, and the bladder (and probably the fish) would simply explode. So instead of having a swim bladder, the blobfish has gooey flesh that is slightly less dense than water. It's a simple solution, allowing the fish to float above the sea bottom as if it were wearing a life jacket.

SINK OR SWIM—
OR JUST FLOAT?

The blobfish's saggy, droopy flesh means it doesn't have much muscle, which means it can't swim fast to chase prey. So the blobfish simply floats above the seafloor and eats anything edible that appears in its way, such as crustaceans. There might not be huge amounts of food down in the depths. But there is enough for the blobfish, because it has no competition from fish with swim bladders.

UGLY CONTEST

In September 2013, the blobfish was voted the "World's Ugliest Animal" after a global online vote. It was also adopted as the mascot of the Ugly Animal Preservation Society, whose motto is: "The panda gets too much attention."

SIZE

2

POWER

1

STRENGTH

1

AGGRESSION

1

DEADLINESS

1

TOTAL

6

TOXIC TERROR

BLUE-RINGED OCTOPUS

Length: about 4 in (10 cm)
Weight: about 1 - 2 oz (30 - 60 g)
Location: around Australia, Southeast Asia.

With its beautiful color and elegant curling arms, the blue-ringed octopus looks like a pretty friendly creature. But despite its small size, it carries enough venom to kill 26 adult humans within minutes. Its bite is often painless, with many human victims not even realizing they have been stung. In a matter of minutes, however, a human can experience complete paralysis and death. Some who have survived say they were conscious but unable to speak or move. So if you see a cute blue octopus on a beach, don't touch it!

LETHAL TOXIN

The blue-ringed octopus produces a poison called tetrodotoxin, or TTX. Just 3.5 ounces (1 milligram) of TTX can kill a person, so it is one of the most powerful natural toxins known. TTX is produced by bacteria in the octopus's salivary glands.

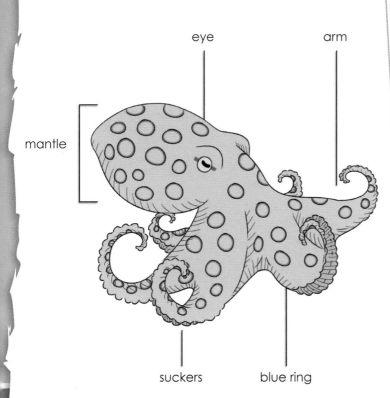

eye

arm

mantle

suckers

blue ring

SIZE

1

POWER

5

STRENGTH

3

AGGRESSION

8

DEADLINESS

7

TOTAL

24

SHAPE-SHIFTING SKILLS

The blue-ringed octopus is so named because its body darkens and the circles on its skin turn a bright blue to scare off predators, such as sharks and moray eels. The effect is like looking at a neon light. This octopus is not aggressive, though—it usually scuttles away if it senses danger. And it can get into virtually any crevice or hole. Like other octopi, it has no skeleton, so it can squeeze into an opening no bigger than one of its eyeballs. It really is the ultimate shape-shifter.

SILENT ASSASSIN

CONE SNAIL

Weight: about 1 oz (30 g)
Length: 4 – 6 in (10 – 15 cm)
Location: Indian and Pacific Oceans and
the Caribbean and Red Seas

Cone snails look harmless. They are small, live in pretty patterned shells, and, like other snails, move very slowly, so they can't chase anything. But appearances can be deceptive. Cone snails are, in fact, ruthless assassins. They can produce hundreds of toxins that they harpoon into their prey. It's instant paralysis and death for their poor victims.

TOXIN TREATMENTS

Modern scientists are making pain-relief drugs from cone snail toxins. They estimate the toxins are one hundred times more effective than the drugs currently used, such as morphine. Prialt is a drug made from the toxins of the species *Conus magus*. The drug is given to cancer patients to treat extreme pain.

FISHING NET METHOD

1 The cone snail has two stalk eyes, a noselike siphon, and a mouthlike proboscis, which all project from its shell. Its eyes aren't very effective, so the snail uses its siphon to smell prey. If it finds a fish, the snail extends its proboscis toward it—the proboscis can stretch to twice the length of its body if necessary.

2 Inside the proboscis is a secret weapon: a harpoon loaded with venom. When the cone snail fires this, the fish jerks rapidly for a second or two and then dies, turning as rigid as a board. The harpoon is barbed, allowing the snail to reel the fish back into the proboscis to be eaten, like a fisherman reeling in his line!

3 Other cone snails use their proboscis like a fishing net. They open it wide so it looks like a tasty sea anemone or a hiding place in the reef. Once a fish has gone in to investigate, the cone snail closes the proboscis and harpoons the trapped prey inside the proboscis bubble.

SIZE	2
POWER	2
STRENGTH	2
AGGRESSION	9
DEADLINESS	10
TOTAL	25

REGURGITATE AND RELOAD

It can take many hours or even days for the cone snail to digest the fish. It will vomit out the bones, scales, harpoon and any sand it has eaten. Then it must reload another harpoon before it can strike again. Luckily, it has around 20 harpoons at various stages of growth, so it always has another weapon to hand.

ANGRY SNAPPER

SARCASTIC FRINGEHEAD

Length: up to 12 in (30 cm)
Weight: about 10.5 oz (300 g)
Location: Pacific Ocean,
from California to Mexico

What's this strangely named creature with the stretchy mouth? It's a fish—and it's called *sarcastic* from the Greek word *sarkasmos*, which means "to tear flesh." And with its huge mouth full of needle-sharp teeth, it can really do some damage. But where does the fringehead part fit in? Well, check out those eyebrowlike tufts on its head.

LIVING ALONE

Sarcastic fringeheads are bitter old loners. Each one lives by itself in a discarded shell, a crevice in a rock, or even in an empty can or bottle—and it doesn't like intruders. This fish sticks out its head to keep a watchful eye out for anything venturing into its territory. At any sign of a trespasser, it flexes and snaps its enormous jaws. If this doesn't scare away the visitor, the fish attacks. Sarcastic fringeheads attack almost anything that appears in their range of vision, including human divers! And their teeth can cut through wet suits. Fringeheads are particularly wary of other fringeheads who compete for the same food in their area. When two fringeheads have a territorial battle, they wrestle by pressing their huge mouths against each other, as if they are kissing. This allows them to determine which is the larger fish. The smaller fish will have to find another home far away from the larger one.

SIZE
3

POWER
4

STRENGTH
4

AGGRESSION
10

DEADLINESS
5

TOTAL
26

6

DANGER IN THE DARK

ANGLERFISH

Length: 8 in (20 cm) to 3 ft 3 in (1 m)
Weight: up to 110 lb (50 kg)
Location: Atlantic and Antarctic Oceans

Ever heard of a fish that goes fishing? No? Well, meet the female anglerfish. She has her own personal fishing rod. It emerges straight out from between her eyes. At the end is a fleshy growth that looks like a nice juicy animal swimming in the water, and it glows in the darkness of the deep. When a passing fish or crustacean takes a bite at this growth, the anglerfish takes a bite at the fish. And what a bite! Her mouth matches the size of her head and is full of long, pointed teeth that are angled inward, so there's no escape. The anglerfish can even extend her jaw and stomach to twice their normal size to gobble up bigger prey.

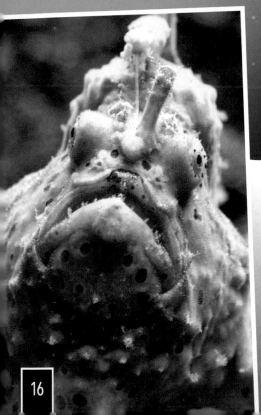

LIVING IN THE DARK

When living things create light, the process is known as bioluminescence. The anglerfish's bioluminescent growth is made by millions of bacteria. The bacteria get nutrients from the anglerfish, as well as a cool place to hang out. And the anglerfish gets luminous bait at the end of her fishing rod—perfect for the dark depths of the ocean. When two organisms live closely together and depend on each other, as the anglerfish and the bacteria do, this is called a symbiotic relationship.

WHERE ARE THE MALES?

When scientists first discovered anglerfish, they wondered why all the fish they captured were female. Then they noticed growths on many of the females and realized these growths were the males. A male anglerfish is tiny, sometimes only 0.25 inches (6 millimeters) long, and when he comes across a female, he bites into her skin and the two become fused together—for life! He loses all his internal organs apart from the testes, which hold sperm. It's a perfect marriage: the male has no need to hunt for food, and the female has a partner to mate with when she is ready to reproduce. Well, it beats searching for a date in the dark, lonely depths of the ocean.

SIZE

4

POWER

4

STRENGTH

4

AGGRESSION

8

DEADLINESS

7

TOTAL

27

PURE MUSCLE

MORAY EEL

Length: up to 13 ft (4 m) (the slender giant moray)
Weight: up to 66 lb (30 kg) (giant moray)
Location: tropical and subtropical seas worldwide

The moray eel is no ordinary wriggler. It has two sets of jaws, each with its own set of teeth. To grab prey, the eel first bites normally with its mouth jaws. Then the throat jaws come into play. They leap forward, bite down on the prey, and pull it straight down the eel's gullet. Why does the moray have a second pair of jaws? The throat jaws allow it to devour large animals within the narrow holes and crevices of the reef. Other predators don't even have room to open their mouths!

PREDATORY PARTNERS

The moray eel has a very special relationship with the grouper fish. The two species form a great hunting team. To get at fish hiding in reefs, the grouper visits the nearest moray and performs a headshaking dance over its home. Usually the eel responds by following the grouper, which repeats the dance over the crevice where prey is hiding. The eel then moves in for the kill, while the grouper waits in the open water. Now there's no escape for the prey: if it hides in the reef, the eel eats it. If it bolts for open water, the grouper gets it.

SIZE

6

POWER

6

STRENGTH

6

AGGRESSION

5

DEADLINESS

5

TOTAL

28

4

ACTING ON IMPULSE

GOBLIN SHARK

Length: 10 - 13 ft (3 - 4 m)
Weight: up to 460 lb (210 kg)
Location: oceans worldwide

If you think this sinister-looking shark looks like a prehistoric monster, you wouldn't be far off. It's the last surviving member of the Mitsukurinidae family, which dates back to the days of the dinosaurs, some 125 million years ago. Often called a living fossil, it's one of the world's most mysterious sharks. It lives deep in the ocean, as far down as 4,490 feet (1,370 m), so few have been caught, and none have ever survived in public aquariums. However, the goblin shark may not be as rare as we think. In 2003, after an earthquake across the ocean floor near Taiwan, more than 100 goblin sharks were found by fishers in just a few days.

A SIXTH SENSE

Appearances can be deceptive. The goblin shark's snout might look like a fearsome sword, but it's actually soft and rubbery. It would be pretty useless in a fight, or even for digging around in sand, but it's very good at detecting prey. It is packed with sensors (called the ampullae of Lorenzini) that can sense the electrical fields that all animals give off. So, even though the goblin shark lives in the darkness of the deep ocean, it has no problem tracking down its next meal. It can even sense fish or crustaceans buried in the sand or squid hidden in ink clouds.

HAMMERHEAD

Like the goblin shark, the hammerhead shark (*right*) also has a snout packed with special sensors that can detect the electrical fields of other animals. But the hammerhead's sensors are packed across a wide, mallet-shaped snout, not a pointed one. This means it can scan large areas quickly, which is perfect for finding tasty stingrays hidden in the sand at the bottom of the ocean.

SIZE
7

POWER
5

STRENGTH
5

AGGRESSION
8

DEADLINESS
7

TOTAL
32

A VACUUM LUNCH

The goblin shark has a unique way of catching its prey. Its jaws catapult forward suddenly, stretching almost to the end of its snout. And as the jaws open, the throat expands too. This creates a suction force that can vacuum up all but the strongest-swimming prey.

TENTACLED TYRANT

GIANT SQUID

Length: 33 ft (10 m)
Weight: 440 lb (200 kg)
Location: oceans worldwide

No one has ever seen a fight between a sperm whale and a giant squid, but we know they happen because the beaks of giant squids have been found in the stomachs of dead sperm whales. And we know that the two animals must have violent battles, because sperm whales are often covered with the sucker marks and bite wounds from giant squids.

BELLYACHE

A sperm whale eats all parts of a giant squid—except for the beak, which is too hard to digest. To get rid of the beak, the sperm whale produces ambergris. This is a slick, waxy substance that coats the beak and lets the whale safely vomit it up or poop it out. But it doesn't always work: 18,000 squid beaks were found in the stomach of one dead whale!

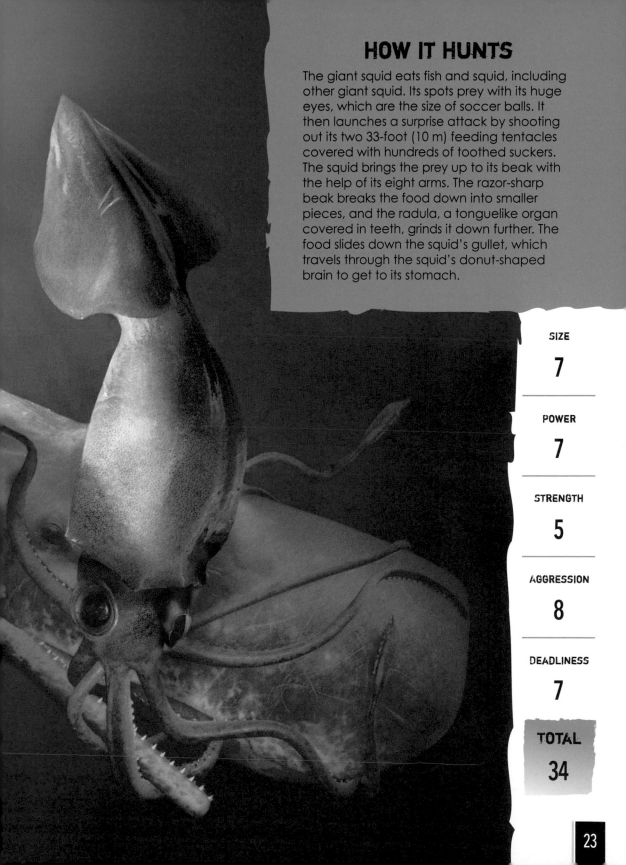

HOW IT HUNTS

The giant squid eats fish and squid, including other giant squid. Its spots prey with its huge eyes, which are the size of soccer balls. It then launches a surprise attack by shooting out its two 33-foot (10 m) feeding tentacles covered with hundreds of toothed suckers. The squid brings the prey up to its beak with the help of its eight arms. The razor-sharp beak breaks the food down into smaller pieces, and the radula, a tonguelike organ covered in teeth, grinds it down further. The food slides down the squid's gullet, which travels through the squid's donut-shaped brain to get to its stomach.

SIZE

7

POWER

7

STRENGTH

5

AGGRESSION

8

DEADLINESS

7

TOTAL

34

GREAT WHITE SHARK

Length: up to 19 ft 8 in (6 m)
Weight: up to 6,600 lb (3,000 kg)
Location: temperate oceans worldwide

Torpedo-shaped and monster-sized, the great white shark rivals the killer whale as the most feared animal in the ocean. Its jaws are about 3 feet 3 inches (1 m) wide and contain about 300 teeth. There are about 48 teeth in the front row, 24 on the bottom, and 24 on the top. Behind those are another five rows, each with about 48 teeth. This means that as soon as the shark loses any front teeth, they are replaced from behind. In its 30-year lifetime, a shark can go through 30,000 to 50,000 teeth.

THE POLARIS

The great white relies on stealth and speed when hunting. One of its most spectacular hunting techniques is the vertical breach. The shark tracks the movement of its prey—usually a seal—by swimming close to the seafloor. While it follows the seal from below, the seal cannot distinguish the shark's gray back from the seafloor. Once in position, the shark suddenly accelerates to the surface, moving at speeds of up to 35 miles (56 km) per hour. If all goes as planned, the shark will take out the seal before it propels itself out of the water. This move has been named the "Polaris" after a famous submarine-launched missile.

SIZE

8

POWER

9

STRENGTH

9

AGGRESSION

10

DEADLINESS

9

TOTAL

45

1 LORD OF THE OCEAN

KILLER WHALE

Length: up to 32 ft (9.8 m)
Weight: up to 22,000 lb (10,000 kg)
Location: oceans worldwide, from the Arctic to the Antarctic

There is only one apex, or top, predator in the ocean, and it isn't the great white shark. It's the killer whale, or orca. It actually attacks great whites, ramming them so they flip over, becoming unconscious and immobile. The killer whale's usual diet, however, is smaller sharks, penguins, sea turtles, squid, and many fish, including rays, salmon, and herring. For a decent-sized meal, orcas often attack sea mammals, such as seals, sea lions, walruses, dolphins, and other whales. Working together in pods, orcas have been known to attack sperm whales, which are also predators but about twice the orca's weight, and even blue whales, which are 20 times heavier. Luckily for us, just about the only creatures they don't have a taste for are humans!

WAVE WASHING

1 You'd think a seal minding its own business on an ice floe would be pretty safe. It's well out of reach of any predators lurking in the water . . . or is it? This seal has not bargained for a pod of killer whales working as a team, using a very clever hunting strategy.

2 The killer whales swim side by side, rising and falling in unison, to create massive waves.

3 Eventually, they will create a wave big enough to topple the seal from its icy perch into the water. Then it's dinnertime.

SIZE	**9**
POWER	**9**
STRENGTH	**10**
AGGRESSION	**10**
DEADLINESS	**10**
TOTAL	**48**

FAMILY AFFAIR

Orcas are not just ruthless killers. They have a friendly side too. They live in pods or groups of six to eighty whales, and they communicate with one another using echolocation, or sending out clicking sounds. Each pod makes slightly different sounds, like humans who speak the same language but with different accents. Killer whales can recognize calls from members of their own pod from several miles away, so each one always knows where its companions are.

MR. BLOBBY

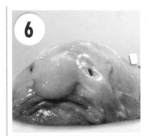

Down in the depths, the blobfish doesn't look quite as blobby as it does out of the water. Its jellylike flesh is held together in a fishlike form by the water pressure of water at the bottom of the ocean.

LITTERBUG

The blue-ringed octopus litters the area in front of its nest with the shells and hollowed-out legs of crustaceans it has eaten. It may put its trash out— but unfortunately, in the ocean there are no garbage collectors to take it away!

GONE FISHING

The anglerfish's fishing rod is called an *illicium* and the fleshy growth at the end is called an *esca*. In some species, the illicium can be four or five times longer than the fish itself.

SMALL IS BEAUTIFUL

About two hundred species of moray eel exist. The smallest moray is thought to be Snyder's moray, which grows to be only 4.5 inches (11.5 centimeters). It lives in the Pacific Ocean.

BABY SHARKS

A baby shark is called a pup. It grows from a fertilized egg that hatches in the mother's womb, where it feeds on unfertilized eggs. When the pup is born, it is about 5 feet (1.5 m) long and can immediately swim away from its mother and hunt for small marine animals on its own. Great whites don't reach maturity until ten to fifteen years, and they can live as long as seventy years.

COME OUT OF YOUR SHELL

Some cone snails attack other mollusks instead of fish. Their venom makes the prey's muscles floppy, so the prey slips out of its shell and can be eaten easily. Other cone snails eat only worms. They are known as vermivores.

SURPRISE ATTACKS

Fringeheads are ambush predators, jumping out from their homes to surprise prey crawling or swimming by. The fish's huge mouth also allows it to eat animals nearly twice its own size, including octopi.

AMBUSH PREDATOR

The goblin shark is not a fast swimmer, so scientists think it may be an ambush predator. Thanks to its low-density flesh and large oily liver, it can drift toward its prey without much movement and therefore it avoids detection.

BIGGER THAN A GIANT?

Scientists first found colossal squids in the stomachs of dead sperm whales deep in the ocean. A specimen caught off Antarctica in 2007 weighed 1,091 pounds (495 kilograms), the heaviest squid ever found.

CAPTIVE KILLERS

In many countries, including the United States, Japan, and Russia, orcas are held in captivity. Many people say this is cruel because their tanks are small and nothing like their natural habitat. Orcas in captivity often act aggressively toward themselves, other orcas, and humans. Critics point out that most orcas in captivity don't live beyond ten years. In the wild, male orcas can live for thirty years and females for fifty years.

MORAY EEL

The moray eel is actually a shy, secretive creature. It makes its home in small crevices in reefs and only comes out at night. Most species do not have pectoral or pelvic fins on the sides of their bodies, so they are not good swimmers in open water and rarely venture away from the reef.

For this reason, diving companies have started hand-feeding morays so tourists can get a better look at them. Unfortunately, this also means divers occasionally lose fingers, because morays have poor eyesight and find it hard to tell the difference between fingers and the food!

CONE SNAIL

The geography cone, *conus geographus*, which lives near Australia, is the cone snail most lethal to humans and has caused several deaths. Its long, flexible proboscis can reach any part of its shell, which means it cannot be safely picked up by hand. Because the geography cone moves slowly, its paralyzing venom must work quickly. Otherwise, prey might swim away before the snail can eat it. One scientist has put the chances of surviving this snail's venom at 30 percent. There is no cure. It's simply a question of trying to keep the victim alive until the toxins wear off.

GREAT WHITE SHARK

The great white shark has great eyesight for spotting prey. It is one of the few sharks to lift its head above the sea surface to look for prey. This is called spyhopping. The shark also has a strong sense of smell. Scientists think it can smell just one drop of blood floating in 10 billion drops of water! What's more, the great white can tell which direction the drop of blood is. The shark's two nostrils are widely spaced under its jaws. Smell coming from the left of the shark will arrive at the left nostril before the right one, so the shark will respond by heading that way.

KILLER WHALE

Killer whales have various ways of catching their prey. In Argentina, they ride waves up to the shore to snatch sea lion pups off the beach, then roll back into the water on the next wave. Around New Zealand, they blow bubbles at eagle rays and stingrays to flush them out from the sediment on the seafloor.

Pods of orcas blow bubbles when they are herding schools of fish. And they dive under the school, flashing the white of their underbellies to stop the fish from escaping. Once they have fish in a tight bunch, some of the whales might swim through them, thrashing their tail flukes so the pod can feed on the stunned and injured fish. Orcas sometimes also force the fish onto a beach where they are easy to pick off.

INDEX

THE AUTHOR
Matthew Rake lives in London, England, and has worked in publishing for more than twenty years. He has written on a wide variety of topics including science, sports, and the arts.

THE ARTIST
Award-winning illustrator Simon Mendez combines his love of nature and drawing by working as an illustrator with a focus on scientific and natural subjects. He paints a wide variety of themes but mainly concentrates on portraits and animal subjects. He lives in the United Kingdom.

Picture Credits (abbreviations: t = top; b = bottom; c = center; l = left; r = right)

© www.shutterstock.com: 2 l, 5 br, 7 br, 10 b, 12 b, 14 cl, 16 bl, 19 tr, 21 tr, 24 cl, 24 bl, 26 b, 28 tr, 28 cr, 28 bl, 29 tl, 29 tr, 29 bl, 30 tl, 30 b, 31 tr 31 bl.